We'll Ge

By Liza Charle

No part of this publication can be reproduced in whole or in part, or stored in a retrieval system, or transmitted in any form or by any means, electronic, mechanical, photocopying, recording, or otherwise, without written permission of the publisher. For permission, write to Scholastic Inc.,557 Broadway, New York, NY 10012.

ISBN: 978-1-339-02789-0

Art Director: Tannaz Fassihi; Designer: Tanya Chernyak
Photos © Getty Images.
Copyright © Liza Charlesworth. All rights reserved. Published by Scholastic Inc.

1 2 3 4 5 6 7 8 9 10   68   32 31 30 29 28 27 26 25 24 23

Printed in Jiaxing, China. First printing, August 2023.

Bend, jump, lean, kick!
It's time to get fit.
We'll have lots of fun!

This gal can get fit on a track.
She'll dash and dash.
She likes to go fast!

3

This man gets fit on his bike.
The wheels spin and spin.
He'll ride for 25 miles!

See the mom and her tot.
They'll skip, run, and hide.
They'll get fit on a slide.

This woman is 75
and she is quite fit.
She'll swim and will not quit.

This teen can stand on his hand.
He'll get fit with hip-hop tunes.
He can feel the beat!

Can a game make you fit?
Yes! Kick, kick…goal!
It is such fun to get fit.